ORDER FROM
CHAOS

JOHN JACOBSON & CRISTI CARY MILLER

To access audio MP3 and MUSIC PDFs, go to:
www.halleonard.com/mylibrary

"Enter Code"
3884-3516-9459-5444

JOHN JACOBSON & CRISTI CARY MILLER

ORDER FROM
CHAOS

TAMING YOUR WILD MUSIC CLASS

ISBN-13: 978-1-42347-668-9

Published by Hal Leonard Corporation
7777 W. Bluemound Road
P.O. Box 13819
Milwaukee, WI 53213

Library of Congress Cataloging-in-Publication Data

Jacobson, John.
  Order from chaos : taming your wild music class / by John Jacobson and Cristi Cary Miller.
    p. cm.
  ISBN 978-1-4234-7668-9 (alk. paper)
  1. School music--Instruction and study. I. Miller, Cristi Cary. II. Title.
  MT1 J15 2010
  780.71--dc22
                              2010020010

Printed in the U.S.A.

Visit Hal Leonard Online at www.halleonard.com

TABLE OF CONTENTS

INTRODUCTION

How did this happen? The 39 other classes you teach each week go off with nary a hitch. You are cool, composed and professional. You write your lesson plans, submit them to the smiling administrator who loves you, then follow them to a tee and joyful learning ensues. You are a success and you have regularly arranged success for your students. All is right with your world.

Then, out of nowhere on a Friday afternoon, arrives THE class where little goes as you planned! The class period of twenty-five minutes seems like four hours and nobody, not you, your loving administration, the PTA and especially the students, are "joyfully learning." What happened? Real life. That's what.

YOU'RE THE TEACHER AND, NO MATTER THE OBSTACLES, YOU TEACH. THOSE RASCALS DESERVE NO LESS.

Every class full of students is unique and not all of them got your September memo regarding proper school behavior and how this ol' classroom of yours is going to work. Sometimes you get a few rascals. Sometimes you get a whole classroom of rascals, and when you do, school can lose it's cool for you and all involved. Now, here's the kicker. You are the one who has to do something about it! You're the adult. You're the teacher and, no matter the obstacles, no matter the challenges, you teach. Those rascals deserve no less.

However, you're better at it than you think, and you're not the first person who has ever inherited the wild ones. In fact, we can hardly imagine a teacher who hasn't, at least once in their career, had a class full of students that made them consider why they chose this honored profession and wonder when the honor is actually going to show up. In other words, this road has been traveled before. There's hope.

We have spent a lot of time in classrooms, mostly of the music kind. We've handled wild classes with a wide degree of success and failure. More importantly, we have been fortunate to meet and glean from literally thousands of fellow educators who, as teachers do, willingly share their trials and triumphs with us and all who will listen, in order that their own journeys from chaos to order can be replicated in classrooms just like theirs. This book is a collection of tricks, methods and ideas that have been tried and found successful by the very likes of you. We share them now with you all, in the same way they have been shared with us. We make no guarantees. We'd like to, but just as no two children are alike, no two classes full of children are the same. What may work splendidly with one crew may fall flat with the next. Such is the nature of the beast or fifth grader. However, we can assure you that all of the ideas we present in this book have been tried on real rascals, I mean students, and found to work with many of them. Many of the ideas are music related, since that is our personal experience, but we think you will quickly recognize that these teaching tips could work in any classroom, as well as the musical one. We hope that, by offering them to you here, you can add them to your own ever-growing bag of methods and techniques, and they will give you a bolstered arsenal of tools to tame that wild classroom.

When we join with other musicians,
it is unlike any other gathering of humans.
We make something meaningful happen
that often changes our very cosmos in unimaginable ways. It
may very well be the only kind of human gathering
that does so quite as effectively.

Let the singing begin!

John Jacobson, 2010

CHAPTER 1

Your Biggest Assets

Your smile!
Your passion!
Your energy!

That's it. That's the whole chapter. Nothing could be more important in your role as a teacher than to remember these three attributes that you never learned, but were instilled in you when you were born to be a teacher. You were born to be a teacher and your smile, passion and energy will get you through when every technique you learned at the Academy falls flat. When the going gets rough, refer to this chapter; you'll be fine and learning will happen.

◆————————————————————————————◆

That's my teacher, my favorite teacher,
smart and good and true.
Ev'ry creature should meet my teacher,
friend to me and you.

CHAPTER 2
Better than Perfect

The evening news can sometimes be depressing. How's that for an upbeat topic sentence? Yet, there are times in the news when something pops up that is truly perfect . . . something that is, perhaps, even *better* than perfect.

This year it "popped up" in, of all places, baseball. You may have seen the story . . . Armando Galarraga, a pitcher for the Detroit Tigers, pitched a perfect game. This has happened only 20 times in the entire history of professional baseball – a sport that Jacques Barzun famously cited when he said, "Whoever wants to know the heart and mind of America had better learn baseball, the rules and realities of the game."

Rules and regulations, that's what baseball is about; that and records. In baseball, we keep records: 27 batters up, 27 batters down, perfect. But wait, did that umpire really call that last runner who was so obviously out, "safe?" Did that umpire really rob Armando Galarrga of his rightful place in the nearly sacred baseball record books? Yep. What's this? The umpire is now admitting his mistake and apologizing to the pitcher? The pitcher is patting him on the back and saying, "Nobody's perfect," while the manly umpire sheds tears at home plate? The commissioner of baseball is saying the bad call stands? What??

Well, one thing great about professional baseball is that they play almost every day, and every day is another opportunity for redemption; to get right what you did wrong yesterday; to strive again for perfection. So, in baseball, tomorrow and tomorrow and tomorrow, they'll all get another chance to get it right. Perfect.

Thank you Armando Gallarga and Jim Joyce (the ump with 20x20 vision) for showing us how to behave. Wherever did you learn it?

Where did they learn it? I have an idea.

SWEAT THE SMALL STUFF

As teachers, we know that training students how to behave is time consuming. All that patient explaining and cajoling, counseling and behavior management can eat up a whole day. It's a lot easier to take the attitude, "Don't sweat the small stuff." When you see one of them doing something you both know is wrong, no matter how small, you ignore it; you permit it. Warning! Warning! This is *not* a good idea. Believe it or not, children are humans, and as humans, they have the ability to reason.

Experienced teachers will tell you that the time spent "sweating the small stuff" early on in their relationship with a particular student or class full of students, will pay off in spades down the road. I have learned that one of the most important aspects of maintaining a good learning environment in any classroom is that the students do what the teacher tells them to do. Some call it compliance. I call it agreeable. I call it *essential.*

I know what you're thinking, "Yeah right. I'm going to stop everything I have planned every time I witness a behavior that I think is inappropriate and deal with it. I'll never get through a whole song or lesson again." Well, you have a valid point. So, it seems the best

TIME SPENT "SWEATING THE SMALL STUFF" EARLY ON WILL PAY OFF IN SPADES DOWN THE ROAD.

solution has to be in what we spent time on long before the inappropriate behavior occurred. We plan for it and we train our students, leading them to appropriate behavior. In other words, they know from the get-go what will be acceptable in your classroom. They "just do it." They comply because it's a *habit*. You teach them the "small" stuff you want to be a part of their everyday behavior. That all adds up to *big* payoffs when students are doing what you expect them to do, what you have taught them to do, what they know to do with no resentment or even resistance. Perfect.

Music teachers are great at this. They are always giving small directions that, when added up, make a large sum of appropriate student habits: "Line up." "Find your mark on the risers." "Hold your Boomwhackers at your sides." The children know to stop playing their instruments when you hold your hands up, or to stand with their feet together and hands behind their backs when you say "Stand By." These are the small habits they do, because you have *trained them* to do so.

Think how many little directions you give when you are teaching a dance to your class. They put their arm up, step on the left foot, clap their hands, or whatever, and why? Because you told them to, and it's their habit to do what the teacher tells them. You got there by *sweating the small stuff* ... small stuff like saying "Please" and "Thank you," "I'm sorry," "Nobody's perfect." *You* taught them that. This doesn't mean you are some kind of ogre in the classroom, constantly scolding over one small incident or another. It just means that you did your homework and led your class to good classroom habits they do without thinking. Now you can spend your real time in class on the things you really *do* want them to be thinking about, like tone quality and rondo form, for crying out loud!

I don't personally know Armando Galarraga, who threw the perfect baseball game that will never be recorded. I have never met Jim Joyce, the umpire who took it away from him. However, in my head and heart, I am fairly certain that those two role models had parents, teachers, coaches and other mentors in their lives whom, all along the way, "sweated the small stuff" so that when big opportunities arose, they both knew the "perfect" way to behave.

I hope we can all be as effective in our own classrooms, using our music, our management skills and our genuine care for our students to lead them to be these kinds of citizens, in America or anywhere.

Now, let's play ball. Better yet, let's play some music!

WHEN IN DOUBT, SING.
WHEN ALL ELSE FAILS, DANCE!

Here's a song to get you started. It is amazing how some of the most important things you have learned, you learned through music: the alphabet, the names of the States, how a bill got through Congress, Bologna's first AND second name. So too, can students have their own self-worth confirmed through music. Sing this song often with your students. Allow them to perform it for their families and peers, and perhaps its positive message will become a permanent part of their self image and attitude.

The Best That I Can Be!

WORDS AND MUSIC BY JOHN JACOBSON AND CRISTI CARY MILLER

Here we stand, feelin' grand! School is cool, so let's get started!
Don't be late! Celebrate! Ev'ry day's a brand new day!

Look at me! (Look at me!) You can see! (You can see!)
I'm gonna be the best that I can be! *Hey! Let's go!*

Ev'ryone havin' fun! No one here will be outsmarted.
Come along, sing a song! Take a look and you will see.

Look at me! (Look at me!) You can see! (You can see!)
I'm gonna be the best that I can be! *Hey! Let's go!*

Books! (Books!) I'll read 'em by the dozen.
Friends! (Friends!) That's what it's all about!
School! (Cool!) It's got my brain a-buzzin'.
Makes me want to shout, to shout!
(Whoop! Whoop! Whoop! Whoop!)

This is it, perfect fit! Ev'rybody is united.
I'm for you, you're for me. So much possibility!

Look at me! (Look at me!) You can see! (You can see!)
I'm gonna be the best that I can ...
We're gonna be the best that we can ...
Let's all be the best that we can be! *Hey! Let's go!*

Use My Library code on page 1 to access audio
recordings and PDFs of piano and vocal parts.

Three Little Questions

Is it safe?

Is it respectful?

Is it responsible?

Our colleague, Yolanda Gardea, a wonderful music-educator-turned-principal, uses this three-question analysis as the basis for discipline in her school. It works well for elementary, middle school and high school. The students are asked to consider these three questions for every action they take or consider taking. On the first day of school, the older students lead an orientation exercise where the younger students are asked to consider a variety of circumstances that might occur during this school year, i.e. a fight on the playground, a joke to be played, sportsmanship, a classroom activity. With each scenario, they are asked to consider the three questions: Is it safe? Is it respectful? Is it responsible? It will not amaze an experienced teacher that the students generally *know* the answers before this orientation, but framing the rule in the form of these questions helps remind them and even helps self-police themselves as the year progresses. Post the three questions prominently in the school and in your classroom. When a student misbehaves, you will be able to refer to this later and have them evaluate their own performance. Not a bad lesson for adults to be reminded of, as well. In fact, make sure the parents of your students know that these are the main criteria by which behavior will be judged in your classroom. Make buttons that the students wear home at the beginning of the year with these three questions on them. With any luck, their parents may decide to adopt the same criteria at home and all the answers will influence behavior twenty-four hours of the day!

Similarly, another school uses the following criteria by which the students self-evaluate their behavior. When chaos happens, the teacher points to these four prominently posted goals and asks the class which one or ones are missing and causing the havoc that is interrupting the learning environment. The four are:

RESPONSIBILITY • RESPECT • COOPERATION • SAFETY

CHAPTER 4
Have a Plan

There are books and dissertations written about classroom management, behavior management and every other kind of school management you can dream up. There are a lot of differing ideas on the subjects, but, if you read enough of them, observe enough successful teaching and consider your own success or lack there of, some ideas and trends definitely float to the top of the success charts.

One common denominator seems to be that so much of good teaching relies on *good planning*. We've all been in the situation where we find ourselves teaching "by the seat of our pants" for whatever the reason. Most of us will agree, it's not fun for either you or your students, and it's certainly not as productive as a well thought out lesson plan. That is not to suggest that just because you had a plan, everything will go according to that plan. There are no guarantees. However, I *can* guarantee that, without a plan, the result will not be the best it could possibly be. You and your students deserve better.

I have often said that being a good teacher is like being a good gardener. You plant the seeds, till the soil, nurture the plants with love and care, and in the end, grow this beautiful bouquet of flowers, orchard of trees, acres of vegetables and berries. The added bonus for a music teacher is that, when your garden flourishes, you might just get beautiful flowers that also sing!

There is even more correlation between teachers and gardeners when it comes to classroom management that, if ignored, could leave you with nothing but a classroom of weeds. In order to grow a beautiful and productive garden, you have to have a pretty good idea how your garden is going to look after things grow, before you ever plant it. You know that a certain type of plant will grow huge, so you don't plant a Sequoia too close to the house. You know that Morning Glory is very invasive, that English Laurel is deer resistant (ha!), that Hostas like shade. (There, that is all I know about plants.) If you didn't take these facts into consideration, you would never be able to plant a balanced, beautiful and productive garden.

Likewise, education is proactive. *You* decide the curriculum. *You* choose the music. *You* decide *in advance* how the students in your classroom are going to behave. If you don't have this clear image in your mind before you start, you will almost assuredly end up with a classroom that is like a dysfunctional garden. You have to know what a good, organized, disciplined classroom looks like in your mind before you can begin to create it. If you have a clear plan and take the preparatory steps necessary to implement it from day one, the harvest can be as rewarding as a well-tended tomato!

YOU DECIDE *IN ADVANCE* HOW THE STUDENTS IN YOUR CLASSROOM ARE GOING TO BEHAVE.

Teachers, start your checklist.

COURTESY
- ✓ Students will speak with courtesy to me, to other teachers and to each other.
- ✓ I will meet them at the door, greet them politely and they will return a polite greeting.
- ✓ Words like "please" and "thank you" will be expected.
- ✓ Students will listen when I am speaking.
- ✓ Students will listen and wait their turn when another person is speaking.
- ✓ Students will put down their hand when another student is asking a question.
- ✓ Students will show the same respect to a substitute teacher as they do to me.
- ✓ Students will treat visitors or new students with respect and courtesy.

WHEN THE GOING GETS TOUGH . . .

✓ Students will know how to act when they are frustrated.

✓ Students will know how to be good winners and losers.

✓ Students will know how to disagree with me, or their fellow students, with respect and courtesy.

CLASSROOM WORK HABITS

✓ Students will know their assignments and complete them in a timely fashion.

✓ Students will stay on task and work up to their potential.

✓ Students will know and follow the routine of the classroom regarding role taking, seat assignments, taking turns, following instructions.

SPECIAL OCCASIONS

✓ Students will know how to behave in an assembly program and how to treat substitutes.

✓ Students will know how to behave when I am working with a smaller group that does not include them.

This list could go on and on and be as detailed as you need it to be. When you observe a classroom that is well disciplined and functioning in a way that encourages a healthy learning environment, it is not an accident. It is the result of a teacher who visualized what they wanted their classroom to be like and then made the expectations clear from the get-go. They had a classroom management plan that included some of the list above and perhaps many more items. They might include expectations regarding cooperative work habits, how the students will respond to authority (yours and others), and so on. The important thing is that you have a plan for your garden and that your plan helps your students blossom.

YOU SET RULES AND PROCEDURES.

So what are the rules and procedures? Let's make another list. Ask yourself these questions and then make your rules and procedures based upon answers you can live with. You can add or delete from it, but at least it gives us a place to begin our strategy.

- ✓ What do you do when you enter the room? Exit the room?
- ✓ What do you do when we hand out instruments?
- ✓ What do you do before the bell rings to start class?
- ✓ What do you do when the bell rings at the end of class?
- ✓ What is the procedure for going to the restroom?
- ✓ What is the procedure for asking for help? Asking a question?
- ✓ How do we take attendance?
- ✓ What is the procedure for handing out and collecting music or other classroom materials?
- ✓ What is the procedure for mounting and standing on risers?
- ✓ What is the procedure for moving from one class to the next?
- ✓ What is the procedure if you were absent?
- ✓ What is the procedure for making up work?
- ✓ What is the procedure when someone knocks on the door?
- ✓ What is the procedure when a guest is in our room?
- ✓ What is the procedure for a fire, tornado or lock down drill?
- ✓ What is the procedure for standing or moving on the floor?
- ✓ What is the procedure for sitting in a chair?

Expectation Rap
BY CRISTI CARY MILLER

It is often a good idea to have the students help design some of the rules of the classroom, led to those rules by you, of course. For instance, start the year by teaching them this expectation rap that introduces the classroom rules for the year.

Listen! Listen! Lend me your ear!

Here's an Expectation Rap for the music year.

Enter the room quietly and have a seat.

To yourself keep your hands and feet.

Listen carefully to what you hear.

Follow directions throughout the year.

Show respect to everyone.

Work together to make music fun.

Time to start with no delay.

Let's sing, say, dance and play.

When the rap is learned, isolate special words within the rap and have different students play instruments as the words are spoken. This rap is good to repeat when the class starts to lose focus during a lesson. (Grades K-5)

Later you might have them compose their own raps, either to replace the one above or to spell out the consequences when expectations are not met. Let them also have a say in structuring the consequences regarding what should happen when the rules are broken.

Break the class into teams and see who can come up with the best rap. This is cooperative learning, a team effort. However, in the end, the bottom line is this ... *"In all situations, teaming or cooperative learning ... Teachers make the teams and rules ... kids think it's legalized cheating, but they learn and make new friends while real learning happens."* With permission, I'm quoting my brother Kerry, a Superintendent of Schools with six kids of his own; so take his justification of chaos with that in mind.

CHAPTER 5
Oh, Behave!

WHO ARE YOU?

You can't expect your students to somehow "discover" good behavior. You need to lead them to it.

Perhaps the most important teaching tool we have at our disposal is our modeling skills. If we believe this, and I do, let's ask ourselves a few questions to help us be the best models we can possibly be.

How do we present ourselves to our students?

Are we rigid and reactionary?

Are we focused more on being a friend to our students than to being their teacher?

Are we polite? Do we say "please" and "thank you"?

Are we groomed in such a way that our students see that we think what we are doing is important.

Are we consistent in our behaviors?

Do we assume the best in our students?

Are we enthusiastic?

Are we organized?

Are we patient?

Are we respectful?

HOW DO YOU TEACH GOOD BEHAVIOR?

In his excellent book, *With All Due Respect* (Purposeful Design Publications) Ronald Morrish writes, "The discovery approach to discipline does not work." He goes on to say that "Practice is an essential component of learning new skills. It is important for learning behavioral skills as well."

He is so right. Believe it or not, not all children will come to school with the knowledge of how to behave. Shocking, isn't it? Consequently, you have to *teach* them. I also think it is very important to point out that what might be acceptable behavior at home or out in the rest of the world, may not fly at school. Sometimes students, and many times their parents as well, need to learn that "school" behavior is quite a bit different than "home" behavior. If this is going to be a place where everybody has a chance and an environment to be educated, those "school" rules need to be learned, embraced and practiced. That should not be so surprising. We behave differently in lots

"SCHOOL" BEHAVIOR IS QUITE A BIT DIFFERENT THAN "HOME" BEHAVIOR.

of different settings. There are acceptable rules of behavior that are quite different say, for example, when we are at church on Sunday morning and at Lambeau Field in the afternoon. You can't necessarily change the rules that a child may live under at home, but "school rules" of behavior must become the norm. The idea and expectation that the only way you are going to behave in this school is the right way is fair and essential. But if it is to be learned, you need to teach them. How do we do that?

Here are a few ways.

Modeling – You are a role model. When you consistently model appropriate social skills, it rubs off. You must be consistently courteous if you want your students to be. You must be organized, on time, enthusiastic, respectful, well-groomed, on task... in short, you must be disciplined if you expect your students to be.

Assume responsibility – We must assume responsibility for *every* student, even the ones who may not be in your classroom. School-wide discipline must be a school-wide agenda. If a student is allowed to act one way in one classroom and a completely different way in another class, how are they going to learn the boundaries of school discipline? I don't mean to suggest that a child behaves the same in math class as in Phy. Ed., but the rules of courtesy, cooperation, respect, safety, and so on are indeed consistent. If necessary, you may have to lead the rest of your school and administration to this fact. It is not appropriate to disavow all responsibility for a student just because they are not at the moment in your classroom. My friend LuAnn, a wonderful middle school teacher, goes to the mall in the summer to practice her disciplinarian skills on kids riding escalators. Full-time teacher!

Don't punish – I know what you're thinking. "What do you mean, don't punish? How am I going to get them to behave if I don't punish them when they do something wrong?" What I mean is, if acting properly (i.e. being courteous, staying on task, being respectful) is seen as punishment, why would they want to do it? It's better to encourage them to try again, only this time like you want them to do it. Correct them. Then, have them practice the behavior you and they prefer.

Beat them to it – For instance, before you ask the students to get on the risers, demonstrate how you get on the risers. Before a guest visits your classroom, practice how you will greet them as a class; how you will behave while they are there, and so on. Here's a good example for music teachers. If you are afraid of the onslaught of emotions that happen after you post the cast for the school musical or after solo auditions, address the issue before you have those auditions. As an example, whenever I hold solo auditions, I have a frank discussion with all those who are going to audition. I explain to them that there will be no grumpiness, tears, back stabbing, etc. when the soloists are announced. I also appeal to their higher sense of humanity. I ask them, "How good of a friend are you? It is easy to be someone's friend when everything is going wrong in that person's life. You can let them cry on you shoulder and feel good about being there for them. Now, how good of a friend are you when everything goes *right* for your friend; when they seem to get all the breaks, the boyfriend or girlfriend you wanted, the solo you coveted. How good a friend you are *then* is a real test of your character." They get it.

Parents sometimes need this little speech in some form as well. This is especially true when they believe their child has been slighted. You would be wise to have this discussion before the perceived slight, if you want to avoid those letters and phone calls. Treat those parents as your partners in the educational process. They are either going to be "fer ya or agin' ya". If you are proactive, most of them will be "fer ya."

In discipline like any subject in school, students will make mistakes. The formula for helping them learn from their mistakes is universal to every subject, including discipline . . . "Correct. Review. Re-teach. Practice."

IT'S A HABIT

Why do we do the things we do? Why do we look both ways when crossing a busy street? Why do we wipe our feet when entering a building? Why do we open the door for a friend, say "thank you" when someone gives us something or say "hello" when we answer the phone? These are the habits of behavior that we have learned, probably some at home and many of them from the good teachers we had growing up. Likewise, when students act in appropriate ways, following rules, carrying out procedures in a proper fashion, following directions, it is because it's what they always do. It's a habit for them. You teach them those habits.

One of the best ways that I know of to teach the habit of following directions is through teacher-led physical warm ups. As a dance teacher, we do this as part of the routine, but it is great for any classroom and here's why. During a physical warm up that you lead, there are dozens of instructions

TEACH THE HABIT OF FOLLOWING DIRECTIONS.

or directions that you are giving to the students. "Stand with your feet part." "Reach your hands to the ceiling." "Bend your knees." "Touch your toes." "Take a deep breath," and on and on. It's a great way to get students into the habit of complying with your directions. They hardly know what happened, and all are better for it! It can also be a lot of fun, while at the same time getting those endorphins going in the right direction.

Have the students practice following directions. Try this one. You say and do:

Reach your Right hand up as high as you can.

Reach your Left hand up as high as you can.

Again R hand. And then L hand.
Touch your R hand to your L ear.
Touch your L hand to your R elbow.
Touch your R hand to your R elbow.

Gets them every time! Though they laugh, they are learning the habits of listening and following your directions.

THE PLEDGE

Another "game," or call it "gimmick" if you must, I use all the time with classes of all shapes, sizes and ages is reciting the pledge. It's just a way of getting the class to repeat aloud some important piece of information I want to make sure they remember. I have them raise their left hand and put their right hand on their heart as though they are taking an oath. Then I say repeat after me . . .

Teacher: I Promise . . .
Students: I Promise . . .

Then I go on in short phrases reminding them of whatever it is I want them to remember. "I will be quiet when I leave the room." "I will remember to be on the risers at 6:30 for tonight's concert." "I will remember to bring my black shoes and white shirt." "I am valuable!"

At our *America Sings!* Choral festivals where we might have thousands of participants, I use this pledge all the time to get the singers to pick up the litter in the park around them. If I forget to administer this simple pledge, "I promise . . . I will pick up the litter around me whether it's mine or not," you can't believe the difference in our after-festival clean up! All I have to do is lead them to appropriate behavior. They yearn for it.

BE SPECIFIC AND CLEAR

When you are making up the rules or giving instructions, it is very important to be as specific and clear as you can possibly be. That's obvious to most of us. But consider the difference between making a rule that says, "You should use good manners in the classroom," as opposed to "say *please* when you ask for something, and *thank you* when something is given to you," or the difference between "Be early for morning rehearsal," and "If rehearsal starts at 8 AM, you should be in the room ready to go by 7:45." Specific and clear instructions will help everybody do their job better.

BE NICE TO THEM AFTER CHRISTMAS

My father, a school administrator for many years, used to say that the first semester is the time to set the rules and guidelines for the rest of the year. "You can be nice to them after Christmas" was his humorous way of suggesting that if you don't set down clear rules and limits and consistently follow them from the beginning of the year, it will be too late when the students return from winter holidays. I think I would even say that your

THE FIRST SEMESTER IS THE TIME TO SET THE RULES AND GUIDELINES FOR THE REST OF THE YEAR.

authority has to be set up from Day One. Even Day Two might make a long uphill battle in your quest for a disciplined learning environment. Students need rules. Students want rules. *You* set the rules. Sometimes you can include students in process of designing how the classroom will run. It can help them understand the rules better and feel more commitment to those rules. But as a general rule, don't make a game of letting them decide the rules and regulations of the classroom. You're in charge. There will be plenty of areas where they will be able to practice their decision-making process and have choices regarding which road to take. You set the procedures, limits and rules that will lead to the kind of classroom you know is necessary in order for it to be a vivid and efficient place of learning.

EFFECTIVE CLASSROOM MANAGEMENT – IT WORKS!

My sister-in-law Deb, a speech therapist in an elementary school in Wisconsin with two kids of her own (Brett and Kaley . . . or three if you count my brother Kent, the middle school principal and Deb's husband!), emailed me this story about one of the teachers in her school.

Cathy Hoof teaches 3rd grade. She is less than 5 ft. tall and weighs under 100 lbs, and she runs the most amazing classroom I've ever seen. Every morning the kids are greeted with a handshake and a sincere "good morning." Expectations are set on Day One and everyone knows what to do every minute of the time they spend in her room. She speaks in a whisper and NEVER raises her voice. She has the kids trained to look at her when she says "eyes, please" – they all turn their heads. Styrofoam cups hang from the

EXPECTATIONS ARE SET ON DAY ONE.

string of every desk. If you have a question, you set your cup on your desk and keep working – no time wasted with your hand in the air! When issues arise, you can hear her (barely!!) say, "How can we solve this problem?"

We still laugh today about a "problem" Brett had in her class. He missed 1 spelling word all year; it was the word ABOUT, and that was a "problem" she would help Brett solve. I guess missing a spelling word was considered a problem for Brett in her eyes; she sets expectations for the kids and they really rise to them.

She has this control over the most disturbed kids, too. It's amazing to watch! When I volunteered in there, I would have to tell myself to slow down and speak softly. I'm sure I drove her crazy! I'm loud, talk fast and like to spontaneously interact with the kids. That's why I'm the speech teacher and have NO classroom control! She has the kids repeat numerous things orally throughout the day, like rules for recess, hallway behavior, and expectations during work time, like "Writing is thinking and thinking is quiet." She gets 3rd graders to write like you wouldn't believe. At the end of the day, the kids line up in the room and she stands at the door. One by one, she shakes their hands and tells them to have a great night and let's them know she's looking forward to seeing them in the morning. We warned Brett and Kaley that the year in 3rd grade would be the opposite of their home; they both played school well and had a good 3rd grade year!

*You cannot hear
the sound of children singing
and fail to think that
this is a world
worth preserving.*

CHAPTER 6

Routine, Routine, Routine!

PROCEDURES, PROCEDURES, PROCEDURES!

The most important thing a teacher can do to help with classroom management is to set down procedures for everything that happens in the room. There should be procedures for entering/leaving, passing out papers, moving from one area of the room to another, making a circle, etc. Time should be spent at the beginning of the school year introducing and practicing these procedures. Many young teachers feel this is time spent away from music learning when, in fact, it is time well spent, as it will have a direct impact on the class learning for the entire year.

HAVE A SYSTEM!

Having a system is so important. Students, even wild ones, like to know the plan and respond well to a consistent system that helps them know what to expect.

There are several ways to approach the development and implementation of a system that works for you. For instance,

✓ **Post the Agenda** for the day on the board. This doesn't mean you can't change horses, or courses, mid-stream but the students know what to expect and expectations are good.

✓ **Start on time.** This shows the class that you are serious, that you value their time, that what they have to learn and experience is so very important.

✓ **Seating Charts** are a must to help keep order and maintain discipline. This also helps students know their boundaries and helps them with procedures. Consider placing the seating charts in a clear plastic cover. Wipe-away markers can then be used for roll call, assessing, comments, etc. (Grades K-5)

✓ Use a **routine warm-up activity** for when the bell rings. All the students can do it without instruction (i.e. Sing a familiar song, play a nursery rhyme, etc.)

✓ **Special Song** – At the beginning of the year, establish a special song (one with a good steady beat) that, when played on the piano, children know it's time to quietly pass in their papers/music "to the beat" of the music. Procedure for passing (if your students sit on risers): each student sitting at the furthest left of each row, passes his/her paper/music to the student on their right. This student then takes both papers/music and passes this stack on to the next person on the right. The process continues until all papers reach the right ends of the rows. The students holding the papers/music then place them in a stack on the shelf. This keeps papers/music with the minimal amount of touches and helps keep them as new as possible. (Grades K-5)

✓ **Tab Board Roll Call** – If you want a quick way to take roll during your chorus rehearsals, try this. Place cup hooks on a square piece of plywood. The number of students in your choir will determine the number of cup hooks you should use. For example, if you have a choir of 25 students, place 5 columns containing 5 cup hooks in each. This will make a total of 25 cup hooks. Next, purchase white sales tags from an office equipment store (or any large department store). Have students write their first and last names on one side of the "tab." On the opposite side, they may place a design of their choice, i.e. flower, favorite football team name, etc. All tabs are placed on the board with the name side showing. When children come in for rehearsal, they go to the tab board and flip their tab so their names are no longer showing. At the end of the rehearsal, all names that are still showing are counted absent. The tabs are then turned back to the name side in preparation for the next rehearsal. (Grades 3-5)

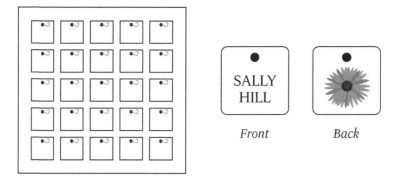

Front　　　*Back*

✓ **Magic Triad** – Nothing works better than a smile, a friendly word and a kind touch. Begin each class period by standing at your door and greeting your students. Let them know that each one is important. (A touch can be as simple as a handshake or "high five.") (Grades K-5)

✓ **Be proactive.** Think of problems before they happen and develop a procedure to prevent the outcome from being negative.

✓ **Be consistent.** Do what you say you are going to do. Follow the rules you and the students establish. However, don't be mulish. There are times when rules should be bent and ignored. Refer back to Chapter 4, where we all agreed that the teacher is the boss!

✓ **Table Points** – If your students sit at tables in your class, give the tables musical names, i.e. woodwinds, brass, etc. Points are given out to the tables for following procedures, completing work, cleaning up areas without being asked, etc. Tables with the most points at the end of the day/week are awarded special privileges or a prize from a secret stash.

✓ **Shoot for the Stars** – The teacher makes the class aware that class scores are based on how well they do as a class. Daily scores are given from 1-5 for the five points of a star. When a class achieves a five point star day, the teacher puts a star on that class' chart. When a certain number of stars are achieved, that class can play music bingo, watch a music video or some other special privilege.

✓ **Sticker Chart** – The teacher places 3 smiley faces (or other symbol) on the board at the beginning of class. Faces can be added for class good behavior. They can also be erased randomly for not following procedures, being disrespectful, etc. All stars remaining on the board at the end of the class are added to a sticker chart. The first class in each *grade* to finish their sticker chart gets a special music day (game or treat.) At the end of the semester, the *class* with the most stickers receives a special party day.

✓ **5-Point System** – This system is similar to sticker chart. Each class is given 5 points at the beginning of class. Points are removed according to class behavior. The class with the most points at the end of the week/month receives a special music day.

✓ **Pocket Chart Power** – At the beginning of the year, each student (by alphabetical order) is assigned a number. They keep this number all year long. A pocket chart is labeled with corresponding numbers. There are 4 slips of colored paper representing different rewards or consequences that students can receive:

- Positive Purple (for good behavior)
- Yellow Warning (1st offense)
- Orange Time Out (2nd offense)
- Red Logical Consequence (continue behavior problems) – consequences could vary from note to parents, phone call home or apology note to another student.

If you see a child do something good, ask them to place a purple slip into their number found on the chart. Negative behaviors are also recorded this way.

✓ **You Can't BEAT That** – Each class earns "beats" for good behavior/ performance. To earn a beat, students participate, sing individually, stay focused, follow procedures, etc. Classes can earn quarter notes/ rests (1 beat), half notes/rests, dotted half notes, whole notes/rests according to how well they respond/perform. (This also depends on the grade level. 1st/2nd can stick to quarter and half note/rest beats since they might not be familiar with the other notes/rests.) For every activity that takes place in class, classes can earn different beat values.

Beats can also be subtracted for negative behaviors (collectively). At the end of the class, the beats are added (or subtracted) by the teacher and students for a total beat score. (Older students that can multiply are challenged to multiply the beats for a total point score.) Classes in each grade level with the highest number of beats gets a music trophy to keep in their room for a week/month. This is a great activity for reinforcing music note/rest names, shapes and values as well as reinforcing math skills. Although individuals can earn high beat notes/rests for the class through positive behavior or performances, individual negative behavior does not affect the total class outcome. Instead, students having a difficult time in class will have their names written on the board with 3 notes placed beside them. Notes are erased throughout the class period for continued negative behavior. If all notes are erased by the end of the class, a logical consequence is assigned (signed folder, note home, phone call, etc.)

PLANS, PLANS, PLANS!

One cannot over-emphasize the importance of "having a plan" before the class enters the room. We realize that it can be a lot of work to write detailed lesson plans, especially when you're teaching many different grade levels and many classes one right after the other. But, knowing *what* you are going to try to do and *how* you are going to try to do it is essential if time and energy are going to be used effectively and efficiently. We all know it is more rewarding for the student AND for the teacher when the lesson is

**KNOW WHAT YOU ARE GOING TO DO
AND HOW YOU ARE GOING TO DO IT.**

thought out in advance, knowing full well that improvisation will always be your secret weapon. But if you simply "wing it" everyday, your wild bunch will decide that "winging it" is the name of the game and you will have an uphill battle from the start.

One principal told me that, generally, his most successful teachers are those that have plans and stick to them. At his middle school they have 45-minute classes and try to encourage their staff to plan three different types of instruction for each of those periods. For new teachers looking for guidelines, he encourages them to break down those forty-five minutes roughly into:

> 10 minutes – introduction.
> 20 minutes – lesson.
> 15 minutes – practice.

His two final instructions were:

- ✓ "Keep it moving!" Avoid staying at an activity longer than 15 minutes, especially for younger children. They need change, as their attention spans don't last as long as older students.

- ✓ Try not jumping from one concept to another. Stay with a particular focus and group of songs until students feel secure. Remember, children love repetition; therefore you can't seem to do it enough!

What we learn through music,
we don't forget!

CHAPTER 7

"D" for Discipline

As you've probably noticed, most of this book is really about discipline and class behavior, and most teachers have figured out a system of discipline, including reward and punishment that works for them and their class.

REHEARSE IT

Perhaps the most important facet of discipline is to rehearse it. As we musicians know, "practice can make perfect" or more accurately "practice makes permanent" whether it's perfect or not. So, the more the rules of discipline are rehearsed, the more effectively they'll stick.

**PERHAPS THE MOST IMPORTANT FACET
OF DISCIPLINE IS TO REHEARSE IT.**

Say to your students." Let's practice being quiet." If students are having a difficult time being quiet in a class period, say ... "I need you to show me what quiet looks like and sounds like. You have 15 seconds to practice this procedure." Look at the clock to begin the process. If any intentional noise is made within that time, start the count over. (Next time make it 30 seconds, then 1 minute, etc). (Grades K-5)

GIMMICKS OF THE TRADE REALLY WORK!

Peace · When the teacher holds up a two-fingered "Peace" sign, the class is to do the same. Many teachers also have the students put one hand in the air with that "Peace" sign and the other index finger over their closed lips to indicate quiet.

Stand By · Use the "Stand By" position – students hold their hands in the small of their backs with their feet together, chins high and faces smiling in absolute silence. This is as if they are "standing by" ready to do some important activity like ... perform a song! Have the students stand up and wiggle around. Then when you give the command "stand by," they are to see how quickly they can get to that position. It can be a lot of fun and an effective rehearsal of discipline.

Echo Clap • The echoed clap is another great way to get them on the same page as you. You clap "ta ta ti ti ta," they echo it and then go to stand by position.

The key to these kinds of tricks is not to over use them or the students become numb to them and they become less effective.

There will even be times when discipline is required from a classroom that is not essentially chaotic. It's okay. It's part of the learning process. The key for a teacher is to administer it and then get over it, not holding a grudge and certainly not relishing it. But, like parenting, if there is never any discipline expected, there will rarely be any attained. It's our job.

"NO" IS NOT A FOUR-LETTER WORD.

There is probably not a more universally recognized and understood word than "No." Even most dogs understand it; not mine, but most. There are times when it is the most useful word in the school.

Rick Smith, an award-winning teacher and author writes a lot about the effective use of the word "no" for classroom management. He describes the characteristics of an effective "no" as "having no blame, no complaining, no wiggle room." "An effective 'no' has no animosity, baiting, antagonism, waffling, sarcasm, equivocation or humiliation. It is simple, clear, to the point and expedient." (From Rick Smith's *Conscious Classroom Management: Unlocking the Secrets of Great Teaching.*)

Sometimes "no" requires explanation, but that explanation doesn't always have to be immediate. Take it up later. Say to the student, "Talk to me after class, or after this activity and we'll see what we can work out."

OOPS!

This may come as a shock to some of you, but chaos often happens most egregiously when you have your back turned. Imagine that! As a consequence, when you turn around with that spit wad in your hair, you might catch the wrong person with the straw. Once I blamed the wrong student for an infraction I didn't actually see. Imagine that!

If you find that you incorrectly blamed a child for an action they did not perform, apologize to the child in front of the class. This lets others know that teachers, too, can make mistakes, and it shows how to handle the mistakes and sets a good example. The violated student also becomes more empowered by your submission and develops more trust that you are fair to all.

STOP TEACHING THE LESSON WHEN RULES ARE BROKEN.

There are consequences to misbehavior. One consequence is that the lesson you made them excited to participate in is not a freebie. They earn it with their proper behavior – behavior THEY designed when they made the rules.

TRAINING THE STUDENT

✓ Don't ever try to talk over a chatty class. This only makes them louder. Instead, lower your voice or wait for the talking to stop.

✓ Develop an atmosphere of mutual respect. Encourage students to treat you and other students the way they would like to be treated. When a student does something disrespectful to others (like talking while the other student has permission to talk), have him/her look at the violated student and apologize for their disrespect.

DEVELOP AN ATMOSPHERE OF MUTUAL RESPECT.

R.E.S.P.E.C.T.

Perhaps the most important thing to keep in mind about taming the wild classroom is that it's about respect; mutual respect, you for the students, the students for you. If we all agree that learning is the ultimate goal in school, then teachers and students alike need to want to make an atmosphere in which learning has a chance. But what does "respect" mean? How do we teach it? How do we demonstrate it? Indeed, how do we even define it?

"Check It Out" (p. 39) is a little rap we use all the time. Teach it to the entire school. It works great as a review before an assembly program or before you receive visitors to your classroom.

Because we sing,
the world shines brighter!

Check It Out! (It's About Respect)

WORDS AND MUSIC BY JOHN JACOBSON AND JOHN HIGGINS

It's about respect!
(Check it out! Check it out!)

It's about respect!
(Ch-ch-check it out!)

It's about respect!
(Check it out! Check it out!)

It's about respect!
(Ch-ch-check it out!)

Gotta treat my friends like family.

Gotta treat my family like friends.

Treat 'em with respect and
they'll be there for me.

They can count on me in the end.

It's about respect!
(Check it out! Check it out!)

It's about respect!
(Ch-ch-check it out!)

It's about respect!
(Check it out! Check it out!)

It's about respect!
(Ch-ch-check it out!)

*R! There's a reason people
treat you like they do!*

E! Ev'rybody take a chance.

*S! It's so simple and it
all begins with you.*

P! People gotta take a stand.

*E! Even when you think
the world isn't fair,*

C! Come along and check it out.

*T! Take a risk, take a ride,
take a dare.*

*Take a breath of air and
let's shout RESPECT!*

*Check it out! RESPECT!
(Ch-ch-check it out!)*

It's about respect!
(Check it out! Check it out!)

It's about respect!
(Ch-ch-check it out!)

It's about respect!
(Check it out! Check it out!)

It's about respect!
(Ch-ch-check it out!)

Use My Library code on page 1 to access audio
recordings and PDFs of piano and vocal parts.

THE LAST STRAW

The last straw ... is usually phone calls home. If difficult behavior continues, making a phone call home to parents usually works. But don't forget to take "Johnny" along for the call. Having him explain his behavior to the parent helps make him accountable. Begin the conversation like this, "Mrs. Johnson, this is Mrs. Miller. I have Johnny with me today and he's having a hard time in music. I'm going to let him explain to you what has happened." After the student finishes talking to the parent, spend a moment talking to the parent and asking for any ideas the parents have used at home that might help. By letting the parent feel that you are working with them as a team, they understand that your focus is toward helping the child get better and not "tattling" about their bad behavior. (Grades K-5)

One more word about phone calls home to parents. One call well-placed, will spread like wild fire through a class. It may be the only one you have to make for a while, once every other student knows you actually did it to one of their own.

Keep in mind when dealing with parents that it is quite possible they themselves may not have had what they considered a positive school experience. They may still feel resentment about something that happened as they were growing up and going to school. Now, they are being asked to come back to this "unfriendly" place and hear about the misbehavior of their child. They may get defensive and argumentative, and the whole episode could have just the opposite effect you had hoped for . . . but obviously not planned for.

There are a few things you can plan for and do that can really help.

✓ Do your best to make the parents or guardian feel as comfortable as possible. If they have come for a meeting with you at school, don't sit behind a desk while they have to sit in a little chair, for instance.

✓ Treat the parent respectfully.

✓ Be friendly, courteous and enthusiastic about the positive possibilities ahead for their child.

✓ Treat them as your partner in trying to do what's best for their child. Neither you, nor they, are the enemy.

✓ Remember, you all have what's best for their child in your heart.

✓ Listen to them as much as you talk to them.

✓ Don't feel like you have to report every little incident of misbehavior their child has exhibited at school. It is the patterns that are important and the future approach you will both develop to encourage improvement.

✓ Instead of using the conversation to encourage the parent to punish the child for past offences, use it as an opportunity to plan ahead for how we want to help the child's behavior improve in the future. For instance, if there is something you are working on in school like tidiness, or common courtesy, you might inform the parent that is what you are working on with their child and it might be helpful if they could reinforce it at home during that same time period of time.

CONSEQUENCES

How do you deal with that student who truly has been disruptive where disciplinary action is required?

First of all, with proper planning and training so that the students always "do" what you tell them to "do," these incidents should be minimal. When they do occur, the first thing to do in dealing with the students is to refer to the list above as to how you dealt with their parent or guardians. Notice the words that jump out and are equally important when dealing with a student.

✓ Respect

✓ Partnership

✓ Looking forward for solutions more than backward to punishment for past activity.

✓ Listen to the student as well as talk to them.

✓ Do not hold a grudge. They are children; you are the adult.

✓ Be consistent without being rigid. Every incident does not warrant the same response or consequence. Be ready to do what is best *this* time for *this* child.

✓ Be friendly, courteous, enthusiastic about the positive possibilities ahead for *this* child.

✓ Remember Chapter 1:
Your smile! Your passion! Your energy!

Somewhere deep inside me,
there played a simple song.
But only I could hear it;
only I could sing along.
Then one sunny morning,
someone set it free,
And all the notes from deep inside
came pouring out of me.

Who would believe
that this song was in me?
Who could conceive
that it would set me free?
All I needed was a chance,
one opportunity,
A person just like you
who saw the very best in me.

Oh now you hear me singing
and I can hear you too.
I can hear that melody
that's deep inside of you.
We can share our music
and bring our dreams along.
Come and we'll make harmony
while singing our own song!

CHAPTER 8

Embrace the Chaos

Don't be afraid of chaos; embrace it! In fact, "organized chaos" can be very educational. Really! Loud doesn't necessarily mean things are out of control. High energy doesn't mean chaos either. The trick is being able to control the chaos and let it happen on your well-considered terms.

**CONTROL THE CHAOS
AND LET IT HAPPEN ON YOUR TERMS**

THE VALUE OF CHAOS

My sister Judy, a high school English teacher with two exigent boys of her own, shot back a quick e-mail when I told her I was writing this book.

"I thought a little bit about order vs. chaos, and I'd like to speak to the *value* of chaos.

There's a lot of safety in *order*. Most people like to know what's expected of them and want to do well by following rules, directions, expectations. Most teachers favor order vs. chaos. They are happier when things are quiet, when eyes are all forward, when feet are under desks, etc.

Chaos implies nothing is getting accomplished. However, some people enjoy chaos and get more creative in the midst of it. I guess, being a part of chaos gives someone permission to break out of their box. Matthew's (her son, the cellist) science experiment a few years ago tended to prove that people learn better with some music playing while they study. I wonder if more controlled experiments endorse that finding.

I took a series of dance classes many years ago that were so mind-bending. Nothing was choreographed. We spent a lot of time either just thinking or just moving, led by one part of our bodies...very individual and creative. My psyche loves choreography – *organized* choreography. However, what do I remember from all the dance classes we took that summer (ballet, modern, stage dancing, etc.)? I remember that one class when we had to crawl across the circle of dancers being led by one part of our body – different for every person. It forced me to think outside my comfort zone. That class was a little *chaos* in the midst of the *order*.

Concerts would be boring if all that was performed was the same kind of music. We need a little bit of chaos/variety to keep things interesting."

DO YOU GENUINELY CARE FOR YOUR STUDENTS?

A word about that question. Of course, you care for your students. If not, why would you choose to be a teacher and spend everyday with them? But how do you *show* that, and how do they *know* it? How can you care for them and make sure that your classroom is a place of learning?

Showing that you care doesn't mean that you try to be their friend, their pal, their buddy. Showing that you care doesn't mean that you never use the word "no," or lose your temper, or do what's easiest instead of what is best. Children these days have so many choices, so many television shows to choose from, so many computer games, ways to communicate with each other and with strangers, fashions to explore, behaviors to try out, and on and on. Caring for your students means leading them to making wise and safe choices even though other choices might be more expedient or popular.

DON'T GET INTO POWER STRUGGLES WITH STUDENTS, BECAUSE YOU WILL NEVER WIN.

I sent out another e-mail to my family (all a bunch of teachers and great resources) and asked them for their ideas on classroom management.

A new teacher in the family, my niece Claire sent me this e-mail. I warn you. She's blunt.

"I have to say, although this is only my second year, this is the toughest one that I have had! Actually, the seasoned teachers say that about this year, as well. I have my mother's ex student, along with a whole mess of EBD and other psycho students. You may think I'm exaggerating, but let's just say, we have had 2 kids expelled and many suspended in and out of school each week. The only way I have been able to survive (and barely) has been that the students and I truly care about each other. I try to let them into my life;

and in turn, they have let me into theirs, and I don't get into power struggles with my students, because you will never win.

Best classroom management is caring and letting them know you refuse to *not* care. I know, only two years here, but that is what I have to offer. Take it or leave it!"

Claire

Ya gotta love it!

Claire's mom (my sister Sherry, recently retired after 32 years of teaching elementary school) followed up with this.

"You are so right, Claire. That is VERY effective in my school. When I have had a student giving me grief during class and I ask him/her to talk to me afterwards and I say, 'Why would you do that to me? You know I would never and have never done anything like that to you,' ... we get results."

Mom

Brother Jeff, a high school principal chimes in with ...

"It works where I teach as well ... 'I would never treat you like this.' 'Why would you do this to me?' ... "

I have a favorite line I use when the immediate conflict is over. 'When I introduce you to my friend, what do you want me to say about you? This is my friend _____. He is ____, ____, ____.' OR ... 'What does your grandma say about you when she talks at the coffee clutch?'"

Sherry responded again. Hey, she's retired. She finally has time!

"Oh, yeah, one more thing, John. Keep your sense of humor. I don't care how chaotic the room is, sometimes you just have to shake your head and smile. If there is another understanding adult around, a smile in their direction (with a head shake) is real stress relief. After all, at 3:30 they're all going to be gone."

*'Twas the night before Christmas
and in front of the choir,
the teacher was thinking,
"When can I retire?"*

Deb, the speech teacher writes ...

"Throw in a lot of Autism, little ADHD, Bipolar, Depression, and a handful of pills and I don't know what the heck I'm doing!! (The kids are taking the pills, not me! However, I'm thinking about trying something!) I have some really involved kids that are just plain hard to figure out and the management of them changes daily, if not by the minute! Most seem to like the purple people eater swing where they can zip themselves into a big purple nylon swing and twirl away! I bet you'd like that too, John! OK, can you tell I need SUMMER?!"

Sherry, the retired one with time, responds one more time ...

"Besides all that ... the most challenging kids for me were always the ones that just wouldn't do anything – no output at all. It's easy to ignore them in the classroom, but it just irritates and grinds at me like a canker sore! In

DON'T FORGET TO GET TO KNOW THE KIDS ON A PERSONAL LEVEL

sixth grade, there were 2 kids who I really took under my wing, but NEVER pointed out during class, only on the side. I worked with one of them after school three nights a week, and then I could get something (minimal, though it was) out of him, and actually we had some connection. He eventually was placed in E.D. classroom and sent to Claire's school, where she had him. The other one, I never did really reach at all – he just slid through, but I see he is graduating from our out-of-district alternative school (which is a step beyond our own district alternative school) this spring. His picture was on the front page of the local newspaper this week and he was quoted as saying something like, 'I was having some trouble with teachers so this has been a good place for me.' He was sitting at a computer in the picture."

Brother Kent, a singing middle school principal adds ...
"Don't forget to get to know the kids on a personal level. Although the classroom is a place of group effort and education, nothing will score respect more than the personal interest you show in each individual student as a human being. Know about their family. Know what they are good at so you can ask them about it – the basketball game they played in, the spelling bee they won, the song they sang."

Another niece Amy, a music teacher, of course, gets the last word in this e-mail exchange. She's taught high school music for a several years now.
"I always teach based on the idea that my first job is to teach my students to be caring, intelligent citizens of the planet earth. Second? To love music."

Uncle John responds, "AMEN!"

CHAPTER 9

Don't Do Anything a Student Can Do for You

Students are not your servants. (I do have a teacher friend who swears she hasn't "sharpened a pencil in twenty years.") Pencils, how quaint. None-the-less, look for opportunities to get your students involved. Taking the responsibility and accomplishing a task on their own, even if it is just sharpening a pencil, creating a PowerPoint presentation, or even teaching a portion of the class, can be very rewarding and educational for all involved.

LOOK FOR OPPORTUNITES TO GET YOUR STUDENTS INVOLVED

LEADER FOR A DAY!

Let a student conduct a warm-up activity or one of the songs you have been working on. They take ownership. You take a break!

REMEMBER ...

✓ Don't try to be a buddy to your students; be a teacher first, teaching them respect, self-discipline, values, and what it means to take on responsibility.

✓ Give students choices, i.e. "Would you like to do this activity standing up or sitting down?" "Would you like to start 'sol' on a line or space?" etc. This gives children ownership in the lesson.

✓ Countdown
When asking children to choose a person to take his/her place in a game or activity, count down from 5 to let them know how much time they have to make a decision. By counting down, children are aware of

the seconds remaining and won't spend a lot a time trying to choose the next person. (Grades K-5)

✓ Answer in complete sentences.
When discussing a concept that has been introduced, have students reply using a complete sentence. For example, if you asked "How many children did Bach have?" a student responding would reply, "Bach had 20 children." Yes, this type of response takes practice. (Grades K-5)

LET'S SING AND MOVE!

"F.I.T." is a song that stresses the three most important aspects of staying physically fit through exercise. It's all about Frequency, Intensity and Time! F.I.T. Get it? But, as we stated before, what you learn through music can often become a part of your very fabric. That goes for exercise as well as eating habits, buckling up for safety and being the best that you can be. Get F.I.T. and get your class physically active. This is the kind of organized chaos that pays off in spades, (and pounds!)

F.I.T.

WORDS AND MUSIC BY JOHN JACOBSON AND CRISTI CARY MILLER

F. I. T.! Think F. I. T.
F. I. T.! Think F. I. T.

Gonna get me movin', it's as easy can be.
Yes, siree! I'm F. I. T.! Think F. I. T.

"F" for frequency–how often I get to it.
Sixty minutes ev'ry day really ought to do it.
"I" for intensity; gotta feel the burn.
"T" for time on healthy habits that I learn.

F. I. T.! Think F. I. T.!
F. I. T.! Think F. I. T.!

Gonna get me movin', it's as easy can be.
Yes, siree! I'm F. I. T.! Think F. I. T.!

Get off the couch! Take some time in the sun.
Go for a walk, or maybe go for a run.
Jump some rope or ride a bike with a friend.
To stay fit, exercising's the best time you can spend.

F. I. T.! Think F. I. T.!
F. I. T.! Think F. I. T.!
F. I. T.! F. I. T.!

 Use My Library code on page 1 to access audio recordings and PDFs of piano and vocal parts.

CHAPTER 10
Getting Their Attention

TRIED-AND-TRUE TECHNIQUES

One of the biggest challenges regarding soothing the chaos of a wild classroom is simply getting their attention. Here are a few tried-and-true techniques that may help achieve precisely that.

✓ **Change the set up** of the room. It may seem like a lot of work, but it can be well worth the surprise factor that keeps their attention for at least a day. If you set up changes in your room, be ready for kids to react differently. Meet them in the hall and explain the new set up and procedures.

✓ **Teach from the back** of the room.

✓ Have the class **face a different direction** in the room.

✓ **Noah's Ark**

   If you are playing an instrument and using music stands, sit someplace different, but with your stand/dance partner. (Get it – two x two?)

✓ **Change location of activities** (risers to floor, interactive whiteboard, learning centers, etc.). This keeps things new for students and will help them maintain focus.

WHEN INSTRUCTING, CONSTANTLY MOVE AROUND THE ROOM.

✓ **Move!**

   When instructing, constantly move around the room. This keeps children looking and interested in what you have to say. It also makes you more aware of classroom happenings.

✓ **Lights Out**

   Sometimes simply lowering the lights will redirect the children and get them quiet. (Grades K-5)

✓ With the lights dimmed, **teach with a flashlight** for part of the class.

✓ **Flash the Lights**
If things get out of control, flash the lights in the classroom to get their attention.

✓ **Silent Rehearsal**
Teach a portion or the entire lesson in silence. Even if the class is asked to make noise, you are silent. It's a great attention-getter.

✓ **Play music as they enter** the room, and have them write down three things about the music they are hearing. You don't have to say a word. Just have these instructions on the board as they enter or on a piece of paper you hand each of them as they enter and take their assigned places.

✓ **Call and Response**
Echos are great attention-getters for the whole class or for individuals. You can do this with voice, body percussion (clapping, snapping, stomping) or with instruments.

ECHOS ARE GREAT ATTENTION-GETTERS.

✓ **Singing Questions/Answers**
Train your students to sing responses to your questions. This will not only draw the focus back to the lesson, but also get your students' attention. For example, the teacher sings, "Who is standing straight and tall?" *(Sol-mi)* Children answer by singing, "I am standing straight and tall." Keep repeating singing this question until all attention is given. This tool will not only help with teaching students to sing in pitch, but it also gets their attention and trains them to answer in complete sentences. (Grades K-2)

✓ **Sing your instruction** to them for any particular activity. They'll watch you strangely AND listen.

✓ **Echo Clapping**

A standard attention-getter is for the teacher to clap a pattern and the class to automatically echo back the pattern heard. Try to vary the patterns given to students in order to keep their attention. For older children, start in this manner and automatically progress to the "Layering Game." (Layering Game – teacher performs a 4-beat body percussion pattern that the students echo. While students are echoing the given pattern, the teacher is performing a different 4-beat pattern. The rhythm game then becomes like a round, with the students 4 beats behind the leader. When the students become secure with this activity, I extend it by dividing the class into 2 groups. I start by performing the 4-beat pattern for the first group who performs the pattern for the 2nd group. Therefore, group 1 is 4 beats behind my pattern and group 2 is 8 beats. Now the activity turns into a 3-part round.) (Grades K-5)

✓ **Rhythm Clap**

Here is a variation of the echo clapping attention-getter: When students are noisy and you need to get their attention, start performing a 4-beat body percussion pattern. Repeat this pattern over and over as children join in. Try to make the pattern challenging for the age level you're working with. (Grades K-5)

✓ **Red Hot Word**

Have a new music word placed on the board when the class enters the room (or place it on a colorful note card). At the end of the day/week, after the concept is learned, place the word on a word wall. Encourage students to use the learned words/concepts throughout the year. (Grades K-5)

✓ **Word Hunt**

Brother Kevin, (another teacher) swears that he uses this activity even with college students, but I know it works with younger ones, too. He says, "How many small words can you find in the word *miserable*?" -same -miser (Or use some other 9 - 12 letter word that relates to the topic). Any word will do. If the class is long, try "Supercalifrag ..." Well, you get the picture!

✓ **Transitional Music**

If you need more time between classes (as the next group is entering), consider using a 2-3 minute piece that children can use to listen to as you prepare for the next class, take roll, mark grade book from the previous class, etc. Tell the students they are to be listening and not talking while the music is playing. Encourage students not to move, in order to practice concert etiquette. On the board, have the name of the piece as well as the composer's name, birth date and death date (if applicable). After the song is over, ask questions to guide children toward the concept of the piece. Also encourage creative answers as to the way the music makes students feel, what they saw in their minds as the music was playing, etc. Once the concept of the piece is introduced (pizzicato, woodwind family, march, etc.), hold up a colored note card with the word/concept written on it. (To reinforce math skills, have your older students figure out the age of the composer when he/she died.) During the next several class periods, listen to the same piece again and discuss the concept. Finally, place the concept word on your music word wall for reference throughout the year. (Grades K-5)

ONE LINERS TO BRING KIDS INTO FOCUS

✓ If playing instruments during the class period, say ...

"If you play before I say, I'll take your instrument away."

✓ When students are getting restless or noisy, say ...

"Show me what quiet looks like and sounds like."

"Show me what hall behavior looks like and sounds like."

"If you can hear my voice, clap 2 times."

✓ Before a lesson begins or when you expect a noisy reaction, explain a procedure you want to use and follow it up with saying ...

"I know you will do this correctly because that's the kind of students you are."

SHOW ME WHAT QUIET LOOKS LIKE AND SOUNDS LIKE.

✓ To get students' attention, try call response:

> Teacher says "Rock" and students respond "Roll."
>
> Teacher says "1-2-3" and students respond "Eyes on me." (Wait for response)
>
> Teacher says "Give me 3" and students respond "Freeze, Face, Focus."

✓ Blow a train whistle! Try to find those great wooden ones that really do the trick. Make it the rule that when you blow the whistle, the entire class responds with "All Aboard!" This will get and hold their attention at least for a short ride.

*Young people and music
can change the world!*

CHAPTER 11

KEEPING Their Attention

TRIED-AND-TRUE TECHNIQUES

Once you get their attention, you have to keep it! Here are some ideas:

✓ **Poison Rhythm**

   If students are lined up waiting for the classroom teacher, have them play Poison Rhythm/Melody to pass some time. In Poison Rhythm, the teacher develops a 4-beat pattern (or 8-beat for older students) that children recognize as the "poison" rhythm to avoid during the game. Then the teacher begins clapping various 4-beat patterns (or 8-beat) that the children are to echo, unless it is the poison rhythm. If they accidentally respond to this rhythm, they are eliminated from play. Likewise, if they do not respond to a rhythm that is not considered "poison," they are also "out." (You can play this game as "Poison Melody" or during class time as "Poison Recorder Melody.") (Grades K-5)

✓ **Music Math**

   Here is another idea while waiting in line. With 2 lines of children (boys/girls), have the first person in each line compete against each other using a music math problem you give them. For example, you can say: "A whole note plus a whole note equals how many beats?" The first one to answer "8" is considered the winner. The loser has to go to the end of their line while the winner stays where they were to compete against the next person. If you want to help the classroom teacher, you can also just work on math facts instead of using note/rest values. (Grades 1-5)

✓ **Line Learning**

   If waiting in line for the teacher, have a nearby folder that has various multiple choice music questions on flashcards. Have the first person in each line compete for the answer or have all students raise hands collectively for the correct response. (Grades 2-5)

✓ **Sing** "My Hands by My Sides..."
This add-on song is a great activity when, all of a sudden, you still have a few minutes left of class. It can be done as a rap or sung to the familiar folk melody.

THINKBOXER

HAIRMOPPER

EYEBLINKER

SMELLSNIFFER

TEETHPROTECTOR

CHINCHOPPER

CHESTPROTECTOR

RUBBERNECKER

BREADBASKET

LAPSITTER

THIGHMASTER

KNEEKNOCKER

ANKLEBENDER

FLATFOOTER

TOETOUCHER

My Hands by My Side

My hands by my side and what have we here?
This is my hairmopper, my teacher dear.
Hairmopper ... *(point to hair)*
dooeedickyvondoo! That's what we learn in the school!

My hands by my side and what have we here?
This is my thinkboxer, my teacher dear. *(point to head)*
Thinkboxer, hairmopper ...*(point to head then to hair)*
dooeedickyvondoo! That's what we learn in the school!

My hands by my side and what have we here?
This is my eyeblinker, my teacher dear. *(point to eyes)*
Eyeblinker, thinkboxer, hairmopper ... *(point to eyes, then head, then hair)*
dooeedickyvondoo! That's what we learn in the school!

Add a new body part to each verse.
Continue to point to different body parts using funny words like...

Smellsniffer (nose)
Teethprotector (lips)
Chinchopper (chin)
Rubbernecker (neck)
Chestprotector (chest)
Breadbasket (stomach)
Lapsitter (lap)
Thighmaster (upperlegs)
Kneeknocker (knees)
Anklebender (ankles)
Flatfooter(feet)
Toetoucher (toes)

✓ Anytime, but especially at the end of a class period that has been a little more rough than you had planned, play a clip of music to clear the air. It can be something soothing or something energetic. Just turn on the appropriate music to help guide the class in the direction it needs to go. Control the soundtrack of your room and you control a good part of the learning environment.

✓ **Thumbs Up Thumbs Down**
Do you like broccoli? Would you eat a hamburger for dessert? This is a great game, especially for the younger students. Allow some of the class to come up with questions that the entire class responds to.

✓ **5-4-3-2-1 Focus**
Here's a game that students beg to play over and over. When preparing children for a program, explain that you will be playing a game. If working with more than one class, the competition could be amongst the different classes. Otherwise, it could be boys against the girls or altos against sopranos. When the teacher says, "5-4-3-2-1 Focus," all students look at the teacher. Have the students then sing through a song for the program. If the teacher catches a student looking away, or not holding hands in the appropriate places, not standing correctly, or any action not acceptable for "performance etiquette," the teacher points to the student and says, "Caught Ya!" That student then has to leave the risers or performance area and sit on the floor in front of the children. (Carefully explain before the game begins that anyone "caught" is not in trouble. Instead, they are just eliminated from the performance area until the game is over.) The object in the game is to be the group with the least number of "catch ya's" on the floor. The winning team is awarded a special privilege. (Grades K-5)

Sounds Like Love

One day, one fine day I met a man,
A simple man of unassuming style,
A kind, gentle soul, a heart warm and whole.
His face wore a peaceful, easy smile.
I wondered how this man could feel such joy,
Unsure of the times that lie ahead.
How could this be? What does he see?
With a nod he turned to me and said:

"There's music in the laughter of a healthy child.
There's peace in the fall of the rain.
There's a song in the breeze, hear it dance thru' the trees,
And harmony in a quiet country lane,
In a tree or a river or shooting star,
In the wonder of the sun that warms the land,
A baby's gentle sigh, a mother's lullaby,
In the friendship of a stranger's helping hand.

Look around and see the joy that's there, everywhere.
Look and find the light in ev'ry day, ev'ry way.
Listen to the world around you.
Open your heart and let it surround you.
It's never very far. It's right there where you are.
It's the simple song of life I'm singing of,
and it
sounds like love."

CHAPTER 12
Physical Involvement

One cannot overstate the importance and value of physical activity to help tame the wild classroom. Start each class with physical warm-ups, exercise and/or stretching. Don't worry about looking silly. They already think that, so you might as well live up to your reputation!

ONE CANNOT OVERSTATE THE IMPORTANCE AND VALUE OF PHYSICAL ACTIVITY TO HELP TAME THE WILD CLASSROOM.

SHAKE IT OUT!

Here's an easy one my niece Jennifer (a fabulous music teacher) uses all the time and she swears it works with students of all ages.

Everyone stands and shakes their right hand (preferably at head level), then their left hand, then right foot (not at head level!), then left foot.

Start by shaking each one for 8 counts (everyone counts aloud); then for 4 counts; then 2 counts, then 1. Finish with a clap.

The goal is to get the clap to sound together, followed by silence. No silence = do it again!

And I quote: "Works like a charm and only takes 30 seconds." Jen

THE JELL-O GAME

What to do with a class of wigglers!

When the wiggling gets to be too much for you, or there is not enough of it, take a tip from my sister-in-law Deb, who also teaches, of course! When her whole class of first or second graders gets a little too squirmy, they play "The Jell-O Game."

Have the class stand up with their hands at their side.

Tell them they are "Jell-O," and the Jell-O only jiggles when the refrigerator is closed.

Pretend to shut a fridge door and they proceed to wiggle and jiggle like crazy. No noise though; Jell-O is quiet.

Then pretend to open the door to catch them wiggling and they all "freeze." If they are caught, they are done playing and have to sit down. No one wants to be caught because it's fun to play.

And I quote: "Works like a charm. And, when the kids get older, they still beg for the silly activity." Deb

HEAD, SHOULDERS, KNEES AND TOES

My sister Joan (elementary school teacher) can't say enough good things about this familiar song activity where you touch the different body parts as you sing. Keep repeating, getting faster each time.

Head and shoulders, knees and toes, knees and toes.
Head and shoulders, knees and toes, knees and toes.
And eyes and ears and mouth and nose.
And head and shoulders, knees and toes, knees and toes.

A GAME WITH ONE RULE: NO TOUCHING!

(Anyone or Anything)

Try this activity when you need your wild class to burn off a little energy in a controlled way.

Skip around the room, then walk.

How fast can you walk without touching anyone or anything?

How slow can you move without touching anyone or anything?

Using music, instruct the students to move the way the music moves. Play various recordings or use the piano to create different moods to move to. End with a slow tune to calm everyone down again.

YOGA

Use Yoga moves and deep breathing exercises. They don't have to be complicated, but the more structured and organized they are, the more responsive the students will be.

RELAXATION GAME

The idea is simply to concentrate on relaxing. Start from your toes and gradually move to your head. Relax each part of your body according to the instructions given by you, the teacher.

LOVE
PILES
UP!

CHAPTER 13

Tokens and Tools

PROPS

In show business, sometimes an added prop can make the whole show click a lot better. The wild classroom is no different. For instance,

✓ **Puppets**

Puppets are a great way to get students back on track. Also consider using different puppets to help introduce various music concepts. For example, when asking students to echo sing/clap, use a bumble bee puppet (perhaps named "Hickety Tickety"), maybe a puppet named Melody Mouse when learning a song, a frog puppet for staccato ideas, a bunny for legato concepts, etc. Younger children are fascinated with these make-believe characters and have a tendency to become focused immediately when they come into play. (Grades K-2)

✓ **Let's Use Some Tape**

Having trouble keeping those dancing lines straight or having children line up in the correct spot for their dance rehearsal? Consider using gym tape on the tile floor to mark the spots where individuals stand. Different colors represent different dances. Also, consider using chalk on carpets for learning folk dances in the classroom. Chalk lines are also great for drawing giant staff lines on the floor for games or concept use. (Grades K-5)

POSITIVE REINFORCEMENT: A TOKEN ECONOMY

Okay, call it a bribe if you need to, but sometimes the simplest little trinket or prize can be a huge motivating factor.

✓ **Stickers**

Vow to give out 10 in each class period! (Grades K-5)

✓ **Toys**

Start collecting an assortment of moveable toys. If a class has earned a privilege, allow them to choose a toy to "push" for some quick fun. (Grades K-5)

✓ **"That was easy"**

There is a button that can be found at Staples that when pushed says, "That was easy." When a student answers a correct question, sings a solo, performs a difficult pattern on an instrument, etc. he/she is allowed to push the button. (Grades K-5)

✓ **Opportunity Cards**

When a student does something that warrants a reward, hand them an opportunity card that might be good for "being the first to go to lunch," "being the one to lead an activity," and so on.

✓ **"Gotchas"**

Have special slips of paper with the school mascot or code of conduct displayed. When a student or students are caught doing something good, the teacher hands out the "Gotcha" slip for the child to take back to his/her class. If a child receives a certain number of "Gotchas," he/she may come to your room (or maybe even to the principal) for a special prize or treat. (All Levels)

✓ **Music Magician**

Pretend to have magic powers. Close your eyes and say something like this, "When I open my eyes, I will see a class as quiet as can be! Poof!" When you open your eyes, make a big deal about your magic powers and how great the class is behaving after being "poofed"! (Grades K-2)

✓ **Smelly Stamps**

Younger children love to be pointed out for good behavior. Find some stamps and several different types of "smelly" stamp pads. These pads can be purchased at many educational stores and in a variety of scents such as blueberry, cherry, etc. When a student is caught doing something right, a smelly stamp in placed on his/her hand. (Grades K-3)

✓ **Praise**

Emphasize the positive! Students love to be praised. Pick out a certain student displaying excellent behavior and then make a big deal about your observation. This immediately gets others in line. During a chorus rehearsal while you're directing, say a person's name out loud with a comment about what you see or hear. For example, "Wow, Amy, beautiful mouth shape," or "Curtis, great expression on your face" or even "DeJuan, way to sing that harmony part." These comments let others know that you're watching and listening and recognize individual efforts. This, too, makes others want to do better in order to be recognized. (Grades K-5)

EMPHASIZE THE POSITIVE!

✓ **Music VIP**

Materials needed: canister, strips of paper, pencils. If a student is spotted doing something good during a class period, the teacher flashes a "V" sign with his/her fingers. This is a signal for that student to go to the canister, write his/her name on a paper and stick it in the canister. At the end of the session, the teacher draws a name from the canister and that student becomes the Music VIP for the next class session. The VIP can be responsible for helping to take roll, handing out papers or becoming a special helper. In addition, the VIP can be given a special place to sit, wear a banner across chest, etc. (Grades 2-5)

✓ **Listening Trophy**

Find some old trophies from athletic events or even choral festivals. Redesign the trophies by placing a big ear at the top. Label the trophies 1st Place, 2nd Place and 3rd Place. Work individually or with your specials teams (art, P.E., counselor, media director, etc.) to give out points during the week/month to classes who are able to follow procedures without having to repeat them. (Points can be calculated on a wipe-away chart placed in the room of

each teacher giving points.) At the end of the point period, award trophies at a morning assembly or over the intercom during morning announcements. The trophies are then displayed in the classrooms until new winners are selected.

CELEBRATE GOOD BEHAVIOR

This next song celebrates good behavior and growing up to be a positive contribution to your class, your community and your world. It's a great song to work on toward the end of the school year to celebrate your progress together. As a reward, allow the class to learn the choreography notes that we've included (PDF file on CD) or make up their own routine. You might tell the class to keep the song a big secret. Tell them that they are going to perform it at the end of the year for their other teachers. With its positive message celebrating their growth, that final performance will be rewarding for all involved! Have no doubt that the other faculty members recognized a wild classroom when it exists. When the students demonstrate their progress through synchronized song and dance, all will feel the success!

Look at Me Now!

WORDS BY JOHN JACOBSON
MUSIC BY CRISTI CARY MILLER

Not long ago I was meek. I was shy;
afraid of my shadow and more.
But learning has given me wings to fly
and now I'm ready to soar.

Look at me now!
I'm ridin' higher than a star in the sky
or a kite on a string.
Look at me now!
I'm catchin' fire and I know if I try,
I can do anything!
Look at me now!

I wasn't sure of my own destiny.
I wasn't sure of my way.
But all I have gathered has set me free.
I'm ready to seize ev'ry day.

Look at me now!
I'm ridin' higher than a star in the sky
or a kite on a string.
Look at me now!
I'm catchin' fire and I know if I try,
I can do anything!
Look at me now!

(continued)

(spoken)
I'm hoppin', I'm poppin'
and nothin' will be stoppin' me.
No lyin', I'm flyin'
and tryin' for the world to see.

I'm givin', I'm livin',
I'm absolutely driven now.
I'm grinnin', I'm winnin',
I'm positively spinnin'.
Wow! Hey! Hey! Hey!

(sung)
Look at me now!
I'm ridin' higher than a star in the sky
or a kite on a string.
Look at me now!
I'm catchin' fire and I know if I try,
I can do anything!
Look at me now!
Look at me now!

(spoken) Look at me now!

Use My Library code on page 1 to access audio
recordings and PDFs of piano and vocal parts.

CHAPTER 14
Technology in the Classroom

Technology is embracing our future and your students are the first to know about all the gadgets available for their entertainment and use. What better time to learn how to use these tools and help bring order to your classroom? Yes, it may involve a few of you who are "techie-challenged" to learn a new skill, but understanding how to use this form of communication can make your life much easier, as well as provide your students with an exciting and enticing way to learn.

Here are some ideas on how to use technology in your classroom:

✓ An **mp3 player** (such as an iPod) allows you to download all of your CDs on this device. Having all of your music in one location can make your life so much simpler. It also keeps your eyes facing forward instead of looking for, or loading, a CD.

✓ A **docking station** equipped with a remote control can be used for mp3 player playback.

✓ Use a **digital media player application** (such as iTunes) on your computer for organizing music files, as well as purchasing a song for classroom use. By hooking up your mp3 player to your computer and logging into this application, you can type in a song you are looking for and use it immediately on your mp3 player. You can also create a playlist of songs to use for the week, or for your entire music program.

✓ An **LCD projector** is a type of video projector for displaying video, images or computer data on a flat screen or surface. Use this device to display PowerPoint or Keynote presentations from your computer for school assemblies or lessons in your classroom.

✓ Connect a **USB remote control** to your computer for hands-free slide advancements of these PowerPoint and Keynote presentations. This is also a great motivator to students when they are allowed to use the remote to advance the slides for you.

✓ A large **interactive whiteboard** is touch-enabled and allows you to make your computer lesson into an interactive session. By connecting your LCD projector to your computer and displaying your lesson on this special whiteboard, it becomes a giant computer screen, enabling children to move letters, numbers, symbols, etc. with their fingers. It also illuminates brightly, enabling you to write with multi-colored pens for teaching purposes.

✓ A **scanner** enables you to scan music or children's books to display on your computer or interactive whiteboard.

✓ An **Elmo projector** gives you an opportunity to display images that are not transparent without having to scan them. They are also able to display 3D objects. Use these for quick display of music or books.

✓ The **eInstruction CPS system** is a student response system using wireless connectivity. Use it as a form of quick assessment. It will provide an exciting way to learn for students and provide you with data about student comprehension.

✓ **Garage Band** is a music-writing program found on Macintosh computers. Students become enthralled as they use this software to create their own music. This program is simple and effective to use and will keep students' interest for long periods of time.

✓ **iPhoto** is another program found on the Macintosh computers. It allows you to organize imported photos or pictures found on websites. Use it to create an instrument book with your students.

✓ **Photo Booth** is another Macintosh program. It allows you to take pictures or videos from the webcam built into the computer. Use it for student performances on instruments.

✓ **Groovy Music** and **Midisaurus** are just two examples of computer software programs for purchase that allow your students music learning. Incorporate these into centers for your students. *Groovy Music* is divided into three different age-level programs that can be purchased separately: *Groovy Shapes*, *Groovy Jungle* and *Groovy City*. Each program offers children the opportunity for exploring sounds and creating music using iconic notation. *Midisaurus* works alone or can be connected to a keyboard for introducing basic piano skills. This program develops music fundamentals sequentially and includes animation, games, songs and activities.

✓ A **Superscope** is a digital recorder that enables you to dub voices on top of CDs. You can also change the pitch and tempo for recordings. This machine also makes it easy to transfer cassette tapes and records to digital files.

✓ **Audacity** is free music software that can be downloaded from the Internet. You can use it to record auditions or make recordings of live performances. This program makes it easy to cut and edit tracks. Plug in a microphone to your computer for a clearer sound. After recording the track, export it as an MP3 or WAV file and then use iTunes (or other media digital player application) to burn a CD.

✓ **Create a Technology Team** selected from your students. Use this group to help set up and run sound equipment for your assemblies and programs.

✓ **Websites** can be used to motivate your students. Hyperlink these to your school music website in order to give students access to this at school or home. Here are but a few:

> BBC Orchestras and Singers
> http://www.bbc.co.uk/orchestras/learn/

> Carnegie Hall Listening Adventures
> carnegiehall.org/article/explore_and_learn/art_online_resources_listening_adventures.html

Classics for Kids
http://www.classicsforkids.com

Composer Hangman
http://www.funbrain.com/cgi-bin/hm.cgi?A2=
composers&A3=1&Submit=Play+Stay+Afloat&A1=s

Creating Music
http://www.creatingmusic.com

Dallas Symphony for Kids
http://www.dsokids.com/default.aspx?

Disney Music Fun
http://home.disney.go.com/music/

Fun Brain Instrument Scramble
http://www.funbrain.com/cgi-bin/scr.cgi?A1=s&A2=instruments

Fun Brain Piano Player
http://www.funbrain.com/cgi-bin/nt.cgi?A1=s&A2=0

Fun School
http://funschool.kaboose.com/fun-blaster/music/index.html

Gullah Music
http://knowitall.org/gullahmusic/journey/index.html

Music Express Magazine
http://www.musicexpressmagazine.com

Music Games (Samples of CD Rom Games)
http://www.musicgames.net/play_musicgames.htm

Music K-8 KidTunes
http://www.musick8kids.com/

National Arts Center
http://www.artsalive.ca/en/mus/index.asp

New York Philharmonic for Kids
http://www.nyphilkids.org/main.phtml?

Play Music
http://www.playmusic.org/

Rockin' Recorder
http://studiokay.com/recorder/Homex.html

San Francisco Symphony for Kids
http://www.sfskids.org/templates/splash.asp

Sphinx Kids
http://www.sphinxkids.org

CHAPTER 15

Projects –
Let's Put on a Show!

Everybody, even wild classes full of rascals, needs three things.

Something to do.

Something to love.

Something to hope for.

What could cover this territory more effectively than putting on a show or a program? It's the kind of project that can bring out the very best in students and faculty alike, for when you put on a show there is always something to do, love and hope for.

WHEN YOU PUT ON A SHOW THERE IS ALWAYS SOMETHING TO DO, LOVE AND HOPE FOR.

Personally, we write musicals with certain classes or grade levels in mind. With a hard-to-tame classroom, the motivation for doing a play or musical may be as simple as a diversionary tactic or a motivating factor that will keep them engaged in the class. But as educational writers, even the musicals that are labeled "just for fun" will almost always have some kind of life lesson or moral to them. After all, we are still trying to teach as we produce a show.

CHOOSING THE MATERIAL

Choosing the music, musical, play or program is crucial in capturing and retaining the interest and enthusiasm of the chaotic classroom. Certainly, it's ideal if the program is curricular in nature and helps them to learn something that is actually expected in their class level. There are wonderful musicals available on subjects ranging from the circle of life to the musical adventures of Lewis and Clark. However, sometimes the reason you choose to spend time on a certain project is going to be similar to giving out smiley face stickers and hot chocolate. It's a reward that might encourage them to behave more appropriately during the rest of the class time as well as during rehearsal.

Here's a list of musicals available through Hal Leonard Corporation in categories that might help you select the best project to work on. There are many other projects available, but these are the ones we know the best so, consequently, we feel the most confident recommending. There are new ones added every year, so go to your favorite music dealer's website or Hal Leonard at www.halleonard.com to check them out.

A caveat: It is not always a good idea to categorize these types of productions too narrowly. This is especially true regarding age level and gender appropriateness. A musical that works ideally for one group of fourth graders might work perfectly for a sixth-grade class in another instance. So, these suggestions below suggest the target group we had in mind when we composed the musicals, but should not be seen as limited to that group. You know your students better than anyone. Hopefully this list will help you narrow your search.

CATEGORIES OF MUSICALS

✓ **All School Play, Musical or Revue**
   This generally implies that the musical is ideal if you want the entire school involved. It might also suggest that you have limited full cast rehearsals, so that the many elements of the show are rehearsed separately, but go together quite smoothly when combined with the other classes. In other words, there might be one song for the first graders that is quite simple, one for second grade, and so on, with more sophisticated music for the older students. Often the older students will handle the speaking parts. It probably does not have rhyming dialog. (This is not to say that a single class of students cannot produce these programs.)

✓ **Grades K-3 Musical**
   This type of musical is written with the younger grades in mind (grades K-3), and usually assumes very little dialog, perhaps one line, per

student. Often these programs come with rhyming dialog, and songs sung in unison, for the most part. Length is generally 20-25 minutes.

✓ **Grades 4-8 Musical**

This type of musical is written for a little older age group. It usually does not have rhyming dialog and the subject matter is more appealing to this age level. Songs might include some optional harmony, and the length is generally 30-45 minutes.

✓ **Express Musicals**

These musicals are more revue/program in nature. They do not rely heavily on costumes or props and are designed to be easily accomplished with minimum staging requirements. These shows have about 20-40 lines of dialog performed more like a traditional concert, with 20-40 different students each having one line to say. They are written for a larger age range (grades 1-6), and usually include 5-6 songs, for an entire show lasting approximately 25-30 minutes.

To learn more about any of the musicals listed below and hear audio excerpts, visit **www.halleonard.com/choral**. Type the 8-number product code into the "Search" field for specific titles, and click on the "Closer Look" icon.

All School Musical Revues

I Need a Vacation! #44223089
I Need a Little Christmas Vacation #09970557
It's Christmas, Carol! #09970635
It's Saturday! #08740370
Mighty Minds #09970720
Once on a Housetop #09970081
Paint the Town December #09970467
Santa, You've Got Mail #09970183
Santa's Holiday Hoedown #09970808
'Twas One Crazy Night Before Christmas #09970066
The Xmas Files #09970138

Grades K-3 Musicals

Arf! #09971305

The Bear Went Over the Mountain #09971418

A Bear-y Merry Holiday #09971311

Bugz #09970157

A Bugz Christmas #09971424

The Cheese Stands Alone #09970254

Christmas on Candy Cane Lane #09970143

Dinostars! #09971183

E-I-E-I Oops! #09970085

Forty Winks 'til Christmas #09971042

Go Fish #09970570

A Holiday "Moosical" #09970625

Holiday Zoobilee #09970372

How Does Your Garden Grow? #09970036

Jingle All the Way #09971189

Lemonade! #09970447

The Littlest Reindeer #09970442

Melton the Warm-Hearted Snowman #09970561

Nuts! #09971047

A Penguin Christmas #09970753

A Place in the Christmas Choir #09970197

Spaced Out #09970630

Three of a Kind #09970377

Grades 4-8 Musicals

The Adventures of Lewis & Clark #08740275

The American Dream #09970553

Compose Yourself #09970259

December 'Round the World #09971037

Dig It! #09970236

Dreamcatcher #09970640

The Elephant's Child #09970024

Get in the Game #09970148

Go West! #09970725

Joust! #09971409

A Kid's Life #09971294

The Legend of Polar Mountain #09970366

North Pole Exposure #09970245

North Pole Musical #09971430

Pirates! The Musical #09971150

River Child #09971052

Rock! #09970108

Santa Goes Green #09971156

Santa's Holiday Playlist #09971281

Snow Biz! #09970735

We Haz Jazz! #09970000

Express Musicals

Cantamos Americanos #09970551

Child of the World #09970425

Destination: America #09970903

Get America Singing! #09970865

Gotta Be Jazz #09971131

Heroes All #09970276

Home for the Holidays #09971082

I Have a Dream #09970962

Let's Sing, America! #09970948

Lights! Camera! Action! #09970996

Music and Me #09970428

My Marvelous Magical Sleigh #09971287

My Town, My World #09970900

On the Radio #09970952

The Quest #09971242

Rock and Roll Forever #09971255

A Tree in Tappen Wood #09971240

Walk With Me, Tulitha #09971401

BUDDING PLAYWRITES

Finally, it can be a wonderfully rewarding experience for a class or cast to have the opportunity to write and create their own play or musical. This is a marvelous idea. You might be surprised which student rises unexpectedly to the challenge and the creative process that ensues. It usually works best if you give them considerable perimeters and make it a group effort.

IT CAN BE A REWARDING EXPERIENCE FOR A CLASS OR CAST TO WRITE AND CREATE THEIR OWN PLAY.

The perimeters might include:

✓ Subject matter

✓ Length

✓ Number of characters

✓ Will there be music and if so what type? (Challenging them to work songs into the story that you have already been working on can be a wonderful exercise.)

✓ Rehearsal schedule

✓ How should the dialog be written (rhyming, non-rhyming, improvisational, etc.)?

✓ No single character should have more than a certain number of lines (depending on the length of the show) and every cast member should have something to say.

✓ Set and prop ideas

✓ Casting

Most importantly, always retain ultimate veto power over everything, including dialog, plot, songs, choreography, casting, costumes, EVERY-THING. (Refer to Chapter 4, and the part where you make the rules!) This does not have to be negative. If it is set up as the expectation from the start, you will save any misunderstanding or hurt feelings down the road. Remember, Preparation! Preparation! Preparation!

Also remember your greatest assets we agreed upon in Chapter 1. More than ever, the tackling of a musical with any class, especially a rowdy one, will call upon your consistent and sincere smile, passion and energy!

They are as awesome as the earth,
more glorious than the sun;
your choir!

CHAPTER 16

Motivation

QUOTES

To help empower students, find quotes to place on the wall in your classroom. Here are some examples,

> "Remember, average is as close to the bottom as it is to the top."

> "The difference between ordinary and *extra*ordinary is the little *extra*."

> "If you aren't afraid to face the music, someday you might be the leader of the band."

> "Genius is one percent inspiration and ninety-nine percent perspiration."
> —Thomas Edison

> "Music is what feelings sound like."

> "Do a little more each day than you think you possibly can."
> —Lowell Thomas

Here's one to keep in your desk or day planner next to your lesson plan for that chaotic class.

> "Music hath charms to soothe a savage breast, to soften rocks, or to bend a knotted oak."
> —William Congreve (1670-1729)

"GENIUS IS ONE PERCENT INSPIRATION AND NINETY-NINE PERCENT PERSPIRATION" —THOMAS EDISON

A COVENANT

I believe that there is or ought to be a covenant between you and your students. From them the promise, never spoken, says, "Teach me to be good. Teach me how to behave. Teach me content."

From the teacher the promise says, "I will do my best to teach you appropriate behavior as well as knowledge. I will assume the best in you. I will assume you want to learn."

As a music teacher, I have gone a step further and written what I think is a fairly inclusive creed that I try to live by as a teacher. I'm certain I cannot be credited with all of these thoughts or turns of phrase, but after 30 years, you hear a few ideas and some of them really stick.

The Music Teacher's Creed

BY JOHN JACOBSON

Music is our tongue for truth;
A door to the inner Light that guides our souls.
It is behind us, before us, within us.
It is our work,
our health,
our essential.
Music is the tool we use to help others feel that there is
something Greater around them and in them.
It helps us discover a heart that can love,
a mind that can reason,
a sympathy that understands.

Hence,
I will be honest in my teaching so others can trust me.
I will be strong.
I will be brave.
I will be a friend to the friendly and the friendless.
I will eat well, sleep well and laugh easily.
I will lift others up.
I will look and listen for things around me that merit praise.
I will look and listen for hidden beauties in my students and my peers.
I will toss harmony onto the world.
I will live.
I will give.
I will be, music.

I will use music to help others
to hear as well as to listen,
and to listen to understand.
I will use music to help others

to feel as well as touch,
to laugh more, cry more, share more, see more,
not just to exist but to live...more.

I will use music to help others to be true
and to see merit in the cause.
I will keep my standards high but my eyes closed
to the small faults of those around me.
I will be an "instrument of peace" and joy and light,
and I will help others find genuine joy in each everyday and peace with the
Impossible.

I will cultivate courage, hope, truth, honesty, kindness, strength,
perseverance, compassion, gentleness, discipline, dedication, pride,
humility, wisdom
and most of all love.
I will use music to teach that making a living is not nearly so rewarding
as making a life.
I will use music to help others to look up instead of down.
I will use music to encourage a yearning for
elegance rather than luxury,
refinement rather than fashion,
wealth rather than riches,
giving rather than taking,
life rather than resignation.

I will teach them joy.
I will teach them hope.
I will teach them to be great.
I will use beautiful music to make all ever more beautiful,
and
I will teach all with whom I come in contact
to let their very life be
music.

BOOKS · PEOPLE · WEBSITES

DR. FRED JONES: His focus is on keeping kids active in their learning.
WEBSITE: http://www.fredjones.com

BOOK
Tools for Teaching (Discipline, Instruction, Motivation)

Dr. Fred Jones received his Ph.D. in clinical psychology from UCLA, specializing in work with schools and families. While serving as the head of the Child Experimental Ward of the Neuropsychiatric Institute at the UCLA Medical Center, he developed methods of helping children with severe emotional disorders. He also began pioneering research into classroom management in both regular and special education classrooms.

HARRY WONG: He focuses on keeping kids in a routine.
WEBSITE: http://www.effectiveteaching.com/cart.php

BOOKS
The First Days of School
How to Be an Effective and Successful Teacher

FREE NEWSPAPER
Successful Teaching

Harry K. Wong is one of the most motivating, exciting and dynamic speakers in education today. But, most importantly, his presentations result in positive audience behavior change. Wong leaves his audiences with practical, useful techniques on how to succeed in the classroom. He has given some 3,000 presentations to nearly a half million people in every American state and Canadian province and in South America, Asia, Africa and Europe.

His expertise is in classroom management and student motivation. Although Dr. Wong regards himself as "a plain old classroom teacher," records show that he has been an excellent teacher who shared his success with thousands of teachers internationally. Because of his achievements, Dr. Wong has been awarded the Outstanding Secondary Teacher Award, Science Teacher Achievement Recognition Award, Outstanding Biology Teacher Award, and Valley Forge Teacher's Medal.

During more than 33 years in the classroom, Harry Wong developed methods that resulted in his having a zero dropout rate, no discipline problems, a 95% homework turn-in factor, and the ability to demonstrate master level learning by each of his students. His students won over 200 awards.

RON CLARK

WEBSITE: www.ronclarkacademy.com

BOOKS
The Essential 55
The Excellent 11

AUDIO CD
The Essential Raps!

Ron Clark has been called "America's Educator." In 2000, he was named Disney's American Teacher of the Year. He is a *New York Times* bestselling author whose book, *The Essential 55*, has sold over 1 million copies and has been published in 25 different countries. He has been featured on *The Today Show, CNN* and *Oprah*, and Ms. Winfrey even named him as her first "Phenomenal Man." His classes have been honored at the White House on three separate occasions. Ron's teaching experiences in New York City are the subject of the uplifting film, *The Ron Clark Story*, starring Matthew Perry, better known as Chandler from *Friends*.

LEE CANTER
WEBSITE: www.solution-tree.com/Public/ProfDev.aspx?node=&parent=&S
howPresenter=true&ProductID=SHF087

BOOKS
Assertive Discipline
Succeeding with Difficult Students
First-Class Teacher: Success Strategies for New Teachers and Parents
on Your Side

Lee Canter is a world renowned expert on classroom management. His acclaimed Assertive Discipline program has been the "gold standard" in the field since it was first published in 1976. Known as one of the most dynamic speakers and trainers in education today, he has keynoted countless conferences and has been a frequent guest on noted television programs including *Oprah, The Today Show* and *Good Morning America*. In the last 30 years, he and his staff have trained over 1.5 million teachers. Mr. Canter is a prolific writer having authored over 40 best selling books for educators including the aforementioned *Assertive Discipline, Succeeding with Difficult Students*, and *Parents on Your Side*. His latest work is the groundbreaking *Classroom Management for Academic Success*.

CHAPTER 17

When in Doubt, Dance!

*Music is a light
growing deep inside of me.*

My niece Claire (6th grade teacher) told me ...

"Whenever my students look as though they are tired or bored, we get up and dance for 1 minute! Then they usually get back on track so they don't have to see me dance up front any longer."

She's gonna be a great teacher! She already is.

When all else fails ... SING!

Nothing soothes the wild beast like music and especially music that you are participating in. It's good for car rides. It's good for the classroom. Of course, you'll sing in a music class, but we would encourage regular classroom teachers to sing more in their classes as well. Sing the alphabet song. Sing a song you are rehearsing for an upcoming program or one that the students particularly liked from the last program. Sing a song that's currently on the radio. Sing your multiplication tables. Sing the names of the Presidents. Sing about character traits like honesty, courage and respect. Sing about life. It has a way of bringing us together and moving even the most chaotic classroom ahead in a harmonious way.

Here, sing this song. Reconfirm the song you have inside of you to be the great and dedicated teacher you want to be to *all* of your students, even the rascals. It'll do you well. And let them sing it, too. Help your students discover the song inside of them that makes them worthy of your considerable efforts. It's all good. So why not sing?

I've Got a Song to Sing

WORDS AND MUSIC BY JOHN JACOBSON AND CRISTI CARY MILLER

When you look at me,
you might see nothing's gonna take me far.
Oh, but if you look a little more carefully,
you might see a star.
When you listen up,
you might hear somethin' that'll make your day.
But if you stay and listen, you'll stand and cheer
'cause I've got somethin' to say!

I've got a song to sing,
my very own song to sing.
It's what I'm meant to be.
I've got a song to sing,
my very own song to sing,
in perfect harmony.

And I've been lookin' for a reason,
and I've been waitin' for the season
to take the song I sing
and share the melody with you. La la la ...

When I look at you,
I can see somethin's gonna take you far.
Oh, and when I look a little more carefully,
I can see a star.
Ev'rybody has a song inside.
It's what makes you, you.
So, sing it out loud; there's no need to hide.
You know what to do!

(continued)

You've got a song to sing,
your very own song to sing.
It's what you're meant to be.
You've got a song to sing,
your very own song to sing,
in perfect harmony.

And you've been lookin' for a reason,
and you've been waitin' for the season
to take the song you sing
and share the melody with me. La la la ...

We've got a song to sing,
our very own song to sing.
It's what we're meant to be.
We've got a song to sing,
our very own song to sing,
in perfect harmony.

And we've been waitin' for a reason,
and we've been waitin' for the season
to take the song we sing
and share the melody with you. La la la ...

Use My Library code on page 1 to access audio
recordings and PDFs of piano and vocal parts.

About the Authors

JOHN JACOBSON

In October of 2001 President George Bush named John Jacobson a Point of Light award winner for his "dedication to providing young people involved in the arts opportunities to combine music, charitable giving and community service." John is the founder and volunteer president of *America Sings! Inc.*, a non-profit organization that encourages young performers to use their time and talents for community service.

With a bachelor's degree in Music Education from the University of Wisconsin-Madison and a Master's Degree in Liberal Studies from Georgetown University, John is recognized internationally as a creative and motivating speaker for teachers and students involved in choral music education. He is the author and composer of many musicals and choral works that have been performed by millions of children worldwide, as well as educational videos and tapes that have helped music educators excel in their individual teaching arenas, all published exclusively by Hal Leonard Corporation. John has staged hundreds of huge music festival ensembles in his association with Walt Disney Productions and directed productions featuring thousands of young singers including NBC's national broadcast of the Macy's Thanksgiving Day Parade, presidential inaugurations and more. John stars in children's musical and exercise videotapes, most recently the series *Jjump! A Fitness Program for Children* and is the Senior Contributing Writer for *John Jacobson's Music Express*, an educational magazine for young children published by Hal Leonard Corporation.

CRISTI CARY MILLER

Cristi Miller is highly regarded across the United States as a master teacher, conductor and composer. After graduating from Oklahoma State University, she began her teaching career instructing grades 7-12. She eventually moved to the Putnam City School system in 1989 where she worked in the elementary classroom for 21 years. In 1992, Mrs. Miller was selected as the Putnam City Teacher of the Year and in 1998 received one of the four "Excellence in Education" awards given through the Putnam City Foundation. In 2008, she became a National Board Certified Teacher and in 2009, she was selected as the Putnam City PTA Teacher of the Year. In 2010, Mrs. Miller became a part of the Fine Arts Staff at Heritage Hall Schools in the Oklahoma City area where she teaches middle school music. Cristi has served as the Elementary Representative on the Oklahoma Choral Directors Association Board of Directors as well as the Elementary Vice President for the Oklahoma Music Educators Association. She currently serves as the President for this organization. Along with her teaching responsibilities, Cristi authors and co-authors a column for a national music magazine entitled *Music Express* and was a contributing writer for the Macmillan McGraw-Hill music textbook series, *Spotlight on Music.* In addition, she serves as the consulting editor for *Little Schoolhouse* book series, "Christopher Kazoo and Bongo Boo." Mrs. Miller is frequently in demand as a clinician and director across the United States and Canada with numerous choral pieces and books in publication through Hal Leonard Corporation. She has also been the recipient of several ASCAP awards for her music. Cristi and her husband, Rick, live in Oklahoma City.

HOW TO ACCESS DIGITAL CONTENT

1. To access content in Hal Leonard's MY LIBRARY, go to **www.halleonard.com/mylibrary**.

2. Follow the instructions to set up your own My Library account, so that codes are saved for future access, and you don't have to re-enter them every time.

3. Once you have created your own library account, then enter the 16-digit product code listed on page 1.

4. **Important:** Follow the instructions on the "Read Me First" PDFs for Mac and PC to **properly** download, unzip, open and use these digital lessons.